501 THINGS
TO DO WITH A
ZOMBIE

501 THINGS TO DO WITH A ZOMBIE

J.C. RICHARDS
Illustrated by AARON WAITE

Avon, Massachusetts

Published by
Adams Media, a division of F+W Media, Inc.
57 Littlefield Street, Avon, MA 02322. U.S.A.
www.adamsmedia.com

ISBN 10: 1-4405-0564-0
ISBN 13: 978-1-4405-0564-5
eISBN 10: 1-4405-0722-8
eISBN 13: 978-1-4405-0722-9

Printed in the United States of America.

10   9   8   7   6   5   4   3   2   1

Library of Congress Cataloging-in-Publication Data
is available from the publisher.

This publication is designed to provide accurate and authoritative information with regard to the subject matter covered. It is sold with the understanding that the publisher is not engaged in rendering legal, accounting, or other professional advice. If legal advice or other expert assistance is required, the services of a competent professional person should be sought.

—From a *Declaration of Principles* jointly adopted by a Committee of the American Bar Association and a Committee of Publishers and Associations

Many of the designations used by manufacturers and sellers to distinguish their product are claimed as trademarks. Where those designations appear in this book and Adams Media was aware of a trademark claim, the designations have been printed with initial capital letters.

Zombie
Lyrics and Music by Dolores O'Riordan
Copyright © 1994 UNIVERSAL/ISLAND MUSIC LTD.
All Rights for the U.S. and Canada Administered by UNIVERSAL - SONGS OF POLYGRAM INTERNATIONAL, INC.
All Rights Reserved   Used by Permission
Reprinted by permission of Hal Leonard Corporation

Splatter art © istockphoto / kirstypargeter

This book is available at quantity discounts for bulk purchases.
For information, please call 1-800-289-0963.

"A way of life that is odd or even erratic but interferes with no right or interests of our own is not to be condemned because it is different."

—Supreme Court Justice Warren E. Berger

Introduction

Since the dawn of civilization (or at least since *Dawn of the Dead*), humans have been consumed by the need to combat, thwart, or otherwise alienate our Zombie brothers and sisters (. . . and, in some cases, pets). But in this enlightened age, where hipsters and ex-reality TV stars roam free, it's time we realize that Zombies were once people, too—people just like you, me, your cousin Sandy, your neighborhood postman, your local librarian. Sure, Zombies may be brain-eating, virus-plagued monsters, but don't we all have our faults? My dog snores. I probably don't floss as much as I should. It's time we put down the pitchforks and learned to live with the undead! After all, what's more fun, planning an escape route from a Zombie—or a trip to Disney with one? An anti-undead defense strategy—or a Zombie surprise party?

So, I ask you, *can you* imagine a world where instead of fleeing the reanimated, you celebrate—and learn to enjoy—a Zombie's many redeeming qualities? Really, when it comes down to it, who—or what—can match the living dead's intense and unwavering dedication? Their remarkable resiliency? Toss in a Zombie's ability to assemble (which, by the way, makes them the perfect organizers for home-shopping parties), and why wouldn't you make this creature your BFF?

Now with the hundreds of fun-filled activities featured within these pages (yes, including real-life recommendations from actual Zombies!), humans everywhere can learn to finally embrace the softer side of these flesh-eating ghouls. So whether it's climbing a tree or using a Wii, going to a farmer's market or playing the stock market, get ready to experience what infectious and monstrous fun awaits when you welcome the undead into your life.

J.C. Richards

1. Ride a bicycle built for two

1. Ride a bicycle built for two

2. Sing campfire songs
   (". . . the more we get together,
   the happier we'll be . . .")

3. Thumb wrestle

4. Go to iHop

5. Adopt a pet

6. Join PETA

7. Grow a Chia pet

8. Speed walk

9. Recite all **44** presidents,
   in order

10. Register to vote

7. Grow a Chia pet

11. Have a staring contest

11. Have a staring contest

12. Go apple picking

13. Recycle

14. Freecycle

15. Unicycle

16. Join a book club

17. Hang a picture

18. Get a passport

19. ~~Go to the mall~~

19. Shop online

16. *Join a book club*

21. Pick flowers

20. Go to Canada

21. Pick flowers

22. Replant

23. Give a toast

24. Make toast

25. Do the Sunday crossword puzzle

25. Do the Sunday crossword puzzle

26. Do a word search

27. Host a wine tasting

28. Go to the zoo

29. Go to Walmart
   (your Zombie will feel right at home)

30. Go to a tent revival

29. Go to Walmart

31. Etch a sketch

32. Play hackeysack

33. See a musical

34. Ride in an elevator
(be careful—Zombies like to push
all the buttons)

35. Have a burping contest

32. Play hackeysack

37. Mime

36. Petition for Take-a-Zombie-to-Work Day

37. Mime

38. Throw a sleepover party

39. Create a budget

40. Create a YouTube video

41. Go swing dancing

41. Go swing dancing
    (keep an eye out for flying limbs)

42. Raise chickens

43. Get a flu shot

44. Get another flu shot

45. Go to a pep rally

46. Do the hokey pokey

47. Go leaf peeping

48. Go to Vegas

49. Shop for a mattress

50. Paint a mural

46. *Do the hokey pokey*

51. Move to Brooklyn
     (Zombies really take to city life)

52. Wear skinny jeans

53. Wear a scarf

54. Wear a scarf in 95-degree
     weather

55. Play hooky

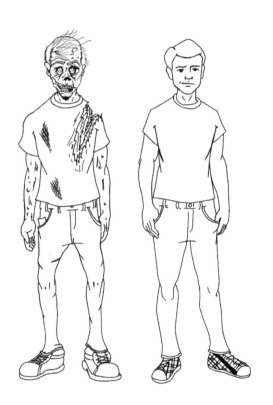

52. Wear skinny jeans

56. Smoke a hookah

56. Smoke a hookah

57. Quit smoking *(Zombies won't mind— or likely notice—if you're irritable, stressed, and eat all the food)*

58. Tell dirty jokes

59. Take a bubble bath

60. Read back issues of *National Geographic*

61. Read back issues of *Gourmet*

59. *Take a bubble bath*

64. Go to the drive-in

62. Move to Queens

63. Join a co-op

64. Go to the drive-in

65. **Get matching tattoos**
(only recommended if you're sure
your relationship will last)

66. **Wait in line at the DMV**

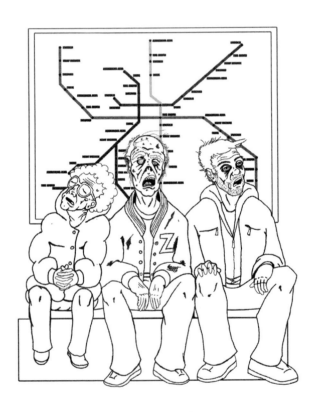

67. Ride the subway

67. Ride the subway

68. Take a Zumba class

69. Watch *Spaceballs*

70. Surf

71. Pretend to surf

72. Get a pedicure

71. Pretend to surf

73. Try tandem skydiving

74. Volunteer

75. Write haikus   My Zombie my friend
                    Used to be the neighbor Bob
                    Now I win at golf

76. Use chopsticks

77. Attend the ballet

76. Use chopsticks

80. *Go to Disney*

78. Watch *Dancing with the Stars*

79. Debate healthcare reform

80. Go to Disney

81. Tweet from Disney

82. Post your Disney photos on Facebook

83. Découpage

84. Play Ring Around the Rosie

85. Ride bumper cars

86. Enter a hot-dog eating contest

87. Look for pictures in the clouds

83. Découpage

88. Go to a tax convention

89. Listen to show tunes

("I feel pretty,
oh so pretty" —
a Zombie favorite)

90. Make a snowman

91. Have a pillow fight

92. Pogo stick

91. Have a pillow fight

95. *Hula-hoop*

93. Do stand-up

94. Host an at-home shopping party

95. Hula-hoop

96. Go through a drive-thru

97. Go antiquing

98. Scrapbook

99. Go to a farmer's market

99. Go to a farmer's market

EAT FARM ANIMAL

~~100. Sing "Old MacDonald Had a Farm"~~

101. Play Chinese jump rope

102. Have dim sum

103. Join Weight Watchers

104. Join the GOP

105. Go sailing

106. Quit the GOP

107. Use bubble wrap

108. Go tanning

109. Get Botox

110. Watch a nature show

III. Work a trade show

111. Work a trade show

112. Visit your grandmother

113. Return overdue library books

114. Moisturize

115. Knit

116. Listen to free-form jazz

117. Play Pac Man

115. Knit

119. *Go to a Renaissance Faire*

118. Join a marching band

119. Go to a Renaissance Faire

120. Go to a toga party

121. Take a walk

122. Go on a hayride
     (unless your Zombie friend has allergies)

123. *Organize a sit-in*

123. Organize a sit-in

124. Baby sit

125. Pet sit

126. Commute
(heavy traffic? bring along a Zombie and
use the HOV lane)

127. Play Simon

128. Play Lotto

129. Breakdance

129. Breakdance

130. Go on a detox diet

131. Work a kissing booth

132. Negotiate a new cell phone contract

133. Volunteer

134. Write a children's book

135. Whistle

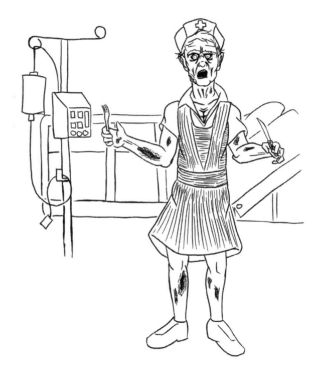

133. Volunteer

136. Karaoke

136. Karaoke

140. *Pick out a gift*

137. Run for office

138. Do the Robot

139. Visit the Natural History Museum

140. Pick out a gift

141. Check out 13 items in a 12-items-or-less line

142. Deny any wrongdoing

143. Make a public apology

144. Further deny any wrongdoing

145. Visit a major attraction

146. Practice the law of attraction

145. Visit a major attraction

151. Go away for a spa weekend

147. Bake a pie

148. Go to a driving range

149. Watch HGTV

(Zombies are really good at demo)

150. Practice viral marketing

151. Go away for a spa weekend

155. Do laundry

152. Participate in a focus group

153. Read *Twilight*

154. Attend a PTO Meeting

155. Do laundry

156. Google

157. Look for the secret toy surprise at the bottom of the cereal box

157. *Look for the secret toy surprise at the bottom of the cereal box*

161. Play croquet

158. Whiten your teeth
(if your Zombie friend
has missing teeth, buy him some)

159. Attend your high school

reunion

160. Wear a polo shirt

161. Play croquet

162. Whittle

163. Watch *Scooby-Doo* reruns

164. Google

165. Build a sandcastle

166. Google some more

167. Learn to play Guitar (Hero)

168. Hug

169. Go on a double date

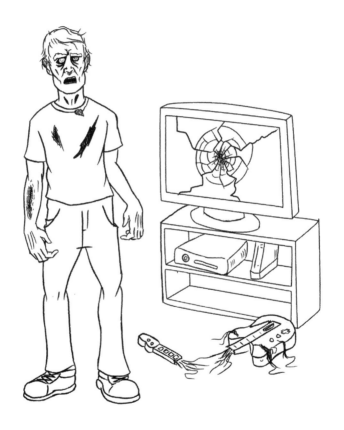

167. Learn to play Guitar (Hero)

170. Enjoy a scenic overlook

171. Solve a word problem

172. Solve a world problem

(Zombies can offer a unique perspective on infectious diseases, population control . . .)

173. Build a bear

174. Go to therapy

173. Build a bear

179. Deliver a pizza

EAT BUNNY:

175. ~~Dress up as the Easter bunny~~

176. Go on an Easter-egg hunt

177. Play Rock, Paper, Scissors

178. Order a pizza

179. Deliver a pizza

180. Make funny faces

181. Brainstorm

182. Chase a storm

183. Lend a hand

184. Cut coupons

185. Spring clean
     (Zombies do windows)

185. Spring clean

186. Go trick-or-treating

186. Go trick-or-treating

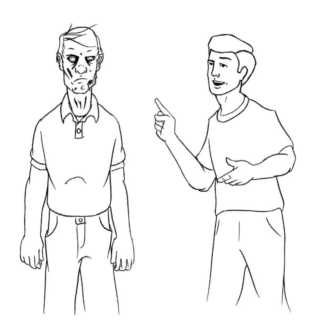

190. Play charades

187. Take a Sunday drive

188. Go to a psychic

189. Go on a cruise

~~190. Play spin the bottle~~
(never mind)

190. Play charades

191. Start a compost pile

192. ~~Run a Ponzi scheme~~

192. Text

193. Cross the street

194. Text

195. Take driving lessons

195. Take driving lessons

200. Carve a pumpkin

196. Text

197. Make up a secret handshake

198. Play poker

199. Get acupuncture

200. Carve a pumpkin

201. Luge

204. *Wear a Snuggie*

202. Live chat

203. Play bridge

204. Wear a Snuggie

205. Start a rock 'n' roll band

206. Fly a kite

207. Join a motorcycle gang

207. Join a motorcycle gang

208. Organize

209. Watch Food Network

210. Make a popover

211. Do a pop-a-wheelie

212. Take a Christmas card photo

213. Record a voicemail greeting

~~214. Pick up a hitchhiker~~ *too risky*

EAT HITCHHIKER

214. Have a food fight

215. Bake cupcakes

212. Take a Christmas card photo

216. Call tech support

216. Call tech support

217. Catch fireflies

218. Jumpstart a car

219. Meditate

220. Refinance

221. Have a yard sale

221. Have a yard sale

224. Bury each other in the sand

222. Go through airport security

223. Go scuba diving
(Zombies don't require certification—

or equipment)

224. Bury each other in the sand

225. Read *Goodnight Moon*

226. Make a time capsule

227. Tap dance

227. Tap dance

228. Have a good cry

229. Go for a checkup

230. Invent an app

231. Play minigolf

232. Attend a cocktail party

233. Invent another app

232. Attend a cocktail party

237. *Participate in a Civil War reenactment*

234. Take a cooking class

235. Try out for the Olympics

236. Try out for a reality show

237. Participate in a Civil War reenactment

238. Participate in a Yankee Swap

241. Sell Girl Scout Cookies

239. Check your smoke detectors

240. Ride a bus

241. Sell Girl Scout Cookies

242. ~~Eat Girl Scout Cookies~~

EAT GIRL SCOUT

243. Get a makeover

244. Study for an exam

245. Participate in a sleep study

246. Play the stock market

247. Play hangman

248. Pay a toll

249. Listen to soul

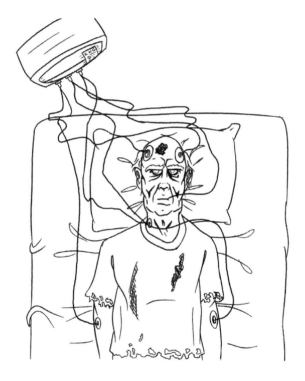

245. *Participate in a sleep study*

255. *Hop on one foot*

250. Belly dance

251. Rush

252. Wear a cardigan

253. Go to Thailand

254. Exfoliate

(a necessary part of any skin-care regimen)

255. Hop on one foot

256. Go to Niagara Falls

257. Watch the PBR

258. Listen to NPR

259. Learn CPR

260. Read Kafka's *Metamorphosis*

256. Go to Niagara Falls

261. Compete in a three-legged race

(this works especially well
with one-legged Zombies)

261. Compete in a three-legged race

266. Have a picnic

262. Watch CNN

263. Start an ant farm

264. Be a movie extra

265. Feed the pigeons

266. Have a picnic

267. Go bathing-suit shopping

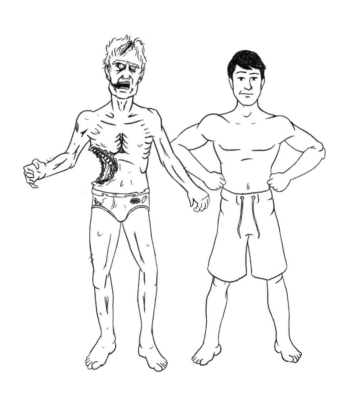

267. *Go bathing-suit shopping*

268. Go to a demolition derby

269. Jury duty
(it's a civil obligation for all undead)

270. Get a deep-tissue massage

271. Have a tea party

272. Go to Starbucks

271. *Have a tea party*

273. Wear a Hawaiian shirt

274. Play catch

275. Make soap

276. Go to a fancy car show

277. Take a Polaroid

278. Ski

279. Wii

280. Play Twister

281. Do a tongue twister
(try saying "Zombie oozes at the zoo" three times fast)

282. Listen—or call-in—to sports talk radio

283. Attend a sporting event

283. Attend a sporting event

284. Go to a poetry reading

285. Sign up for Continuing Ed

286. Make felt handbags with
bird appliqués

287. Learn the Flamenco

288. Sell felt handbags with bird
appliqués on Etsy

289. Remove wallpaper

290. Go to a dog show

291. Go to an all-you-can-eat buffet

292. Make pottery

293. Write a letter to Santa
      ZOMBIE GOOD
        ..WANT BRAIN

292. Make pottery

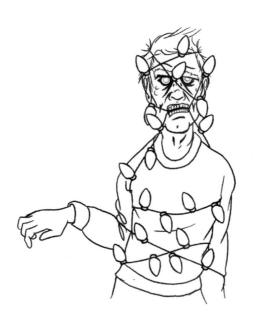

298. Decorate for the holidays

294. Go sledding

295. Bungee jump

296. Wear white after Labor Day

297. Save for a rainy day

298. Decorate for the holidays

299. Hopscotch

300. Skinny dip

301. Double dip

302. Go on a hot air balloon ride

303. Play table tennis

304. Blow bubbles

305. See-saw

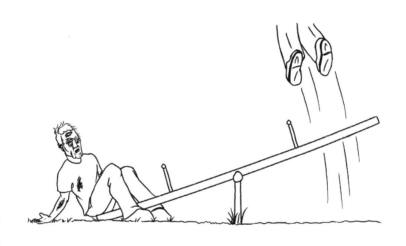

305. See-saw

306. Join a gym

306. Join a gym

311. *Hit a piñata*

307. Celebrate the winter solstice

308. Watch NASCAR

309. Go to a flea market

310. Investigate the paranormal

311. Hit a piñata

312. Play Miss Mary Mack

312. Play Miss Mary Mack

317. Change a light bulb

313. Start a blog

314. Make a family tree

315. Make a model airplane

316. Make up

317. Change a light bulb

318. Play pin the tail on the donkey

319. Go RVing

320. Change a tire

321. Join AAA

322. Go horseback riding

323. Go house hunting

324. Play kickball

325. Grocery shop

326. Make homemade valentines

327. Clap on

328. Clap off

328. Clap off

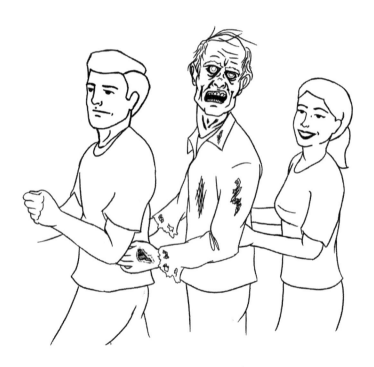

333. Join a Conga line

329. Finger paint

330. Iron

331. Go to Europe
(there's nothing like seeing the
Sistine Chapel for the first time
with a Zombie)

332. Go bowling

333. Join a Conga line

334. Space tourism

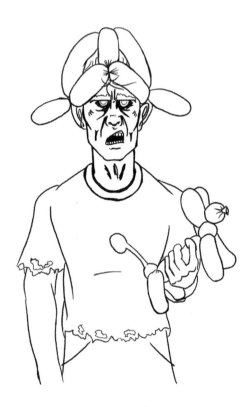

335. Make balloon animals

335. Make balloon animals

336. Go to a water park

337. Go to a concert

338. Sing "Sweet Caroline"

339. Spell M-I-S-S-I-S-S-I-P-P-I

340. Go to the Kentucky Derby

341. Play HORSE

342. Play Bingo

343. Google

344. ~~Save the gorillas~~ YUMMY GORILLAS

345. Use duct tape

342. Play Bingo

346. Collect decorative swords

347. Attend the Academy Awards

348. Ask for a raise

349. Join a club

350. Start a religion

347. Attend the Academy Awards

351. Road trip

351. Road trip

352. Ask for directions

353. Use a GPS

354. Swim with the dolphins

355. Play tic tac toe

356. Google

358. Relive the '80s

357. **Pay taxes**
(check in with your accountant about a Zombie credit)

358. **Relive the '80s**

359. **Slip 'n' slide**

360. **Go through a corn maze**

361. **Run with the bulls**

362. Stay up all night

363. Tickle

364. Design a t-shirt

365. Tie dye

366. Barbecue

364. *Design a t-shirt*

367. Diagram a sentence

367. Diagram a sentence

368. Play Duck, Duck, Goose!

369. Attend a something-palooza

370. Make a dream catcher

371. Make a lemonade stand

372. Make a five-year plan

371. *Make a lemonade stand*

376. Visit an island destination

373. Do the chicken dance

374. Slam dance

375. See *Stars on Ice*

376. Visit an island destination

377. Tour a timeshare

378. Go shoe shopping

379. Swing

380. Tour a swamp

381. Play Freeze Tag

382. Buy a freezer

383. Play blackjack

384. Stay at a B&B

385. Go cow tipping

386. Skip rocks

387. Help proprietors find lost cows

388. Read a newspaper

388. Read a newspaper

389. Play matchmaker

390. Get bangs

391. Plan a surprise party

392. Crash a party

393. Return a gift
   (no receipts, no problem)

394. Re-gift

395. Play lawn darts

396. Program the remote

397. Play doubles tennis

398. Sit 'n' spin

399. Attend a film festival

399. Attend a film festival

400. Wear a blazer

401. ~~Soak in a hot tub~~

401. Yodel

402. Roller skate

403. Sit for a portrait

404. Jump up and down on the bed

403. Sit for a portrait

410. Visit Amish Country

405. Watch an entire infomercial
(just keep your Zombie away from the phone)

406. Inhale a helium balloon and speak in funny voices

407. Learn shorthand

408. Wear Mukluks

409. Make sno-cones

410. Visit Amish Country

415. Do origami

411. Go to a motivational seminar

412. Take an IQ test

413. Save the rain forest

414. ~~Walk a dog~~ EAT DOG

415. Do origami

416. Tug-of-War

417. Make a Dance Mix

418. Get hair plugs

419. Do magic tricks (Zombies are really good at pulling the rabbit out of the hat and making it disappear

420. Make snow angels

420. *Make snow angels*

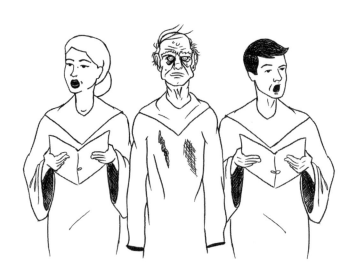

426. Sing in a choir

421. Limbo

422. Geocache

423. Go to a dude ranch

424. Watch a spaghetti western

425. Meet the neighbors

426. Sing in a choir

427. Go to Graceland

428. Go tubing

429. Start an ant farm

430. Walk through a revolving door

431. Take a standardized test

432. Go to the Guggenheim

430. Walk through a revolving door

433. Make shadow puppets

433. Make shadow puppets

434. Yoga

434. Yoga

435. Learn how to golf

436. Quit golf

437. Go clubbing

438. Play Peek-a-Boo

439. Walk like an Egyptian

440. Paint by numbers

441. Share a secret

442. Hunt for bargains

443. Drink green tea

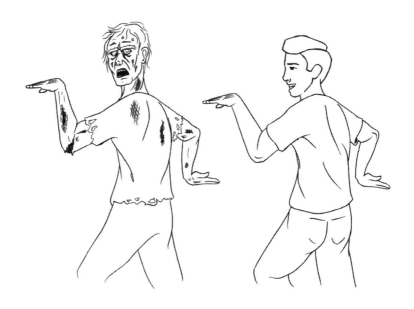

439. Walk like an Egyptian

444. Play hide-n-seek

444. Play hide-n-seek

445. Just hide

446. Change your hair color

447. Take up archery

448. Give up caffeine

449. Get your face painted

450. Floss

451. Grow a vegetable garden

452. Draw a picture of a kitty

453. Look for a missing kitty

454. Learn how to pilot a hot
air balloon

455. Make a resolution

451. Grow a vegetable garden

456. Learn to sail

456. Learn to sail

457. Collect antique swords

458. Look for another missing kitty . . .

459. Enter the Publishers Clearing House Sweepstakes

460. Go to the post office

461. Read *Self-Reliance*

462. *See who can be quiet the longest*

462. See who can be quiet
the longest

463. Wear matching earmuffs

464. Hold an open house

465. Build a tree fort

466. Look for a missing glove

467. Look for a missing limb

468. Take out a life insurance policy

469. ~~Take a nap~~

469. Go for a checkup

470. Earn your wilderness survival badge

471. Read *The Everything® Canning & Preserving Book*

472. Buy sunglasses

473. Rent a U-Haul

474. Go see the penguins at
the aquarium

475. Make a friendly wager

476. Predict the weather

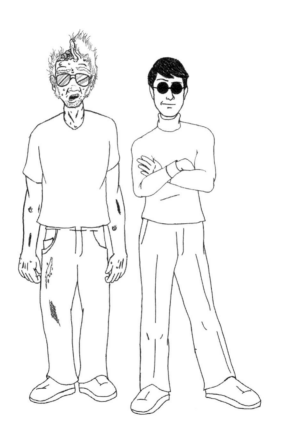

472. *Buy sunglasses*

477. Make cheese

478. Join the NRA

479. Play Operation

480. File an insurance claim

481. Call in sick

477. Make cheese

482. Write a letter

483. Flip a coin

484. Play the bongos, loudly

485. Lift a heavy object

486. Keep a secret

487. Go hiking in the desert

488. Install solar panels

489. Look under the bed for monsters

MONSTER FRIEND

490. Make a living will

491. Write a memoir

492. Learn sign language

492. Learn sign language

493. Visit your mother-in-law

494. Watch sunrise

495. Become an amateur ham radio operator

496. Apply sunscreen

497. Buy a water purifier

498. Make a list

499. Consider rejoining GOP

500. Become a vegetarian

501. Live in the moment

Use the space below to add in your own ideas for living-undead activities.* Hopefully, this book has served as just the starting point for a long future of human-Zombie fun.

502. _____

503. _____

504. _____

505. _____

(*And maybe to note those that didn't work out so well.)

506. _____

507. _____

508. _____

509. _____

510. _____

511. _____

512. _____

513. _____

514. _____

515. _____

516. _____

517. _____

518. _____

519. _____

520. _____

Author's Acknowledgments

A world of thanks to the many people—and Zombies (you know who you are)—who made this simple dream of promoting subhuman rights a reality:

John, Jack, and Chi Chi who clearly know how to have fun with anyone—living or undead.

The great minds at Adams Media, including Wendy Simard, Matt Glazer, Paula Munier, Meredith O'Hayre, and the rest of the editorial team who recognized and supported the need for this book. The design team of Frank Rivera and Colleen Cunningham. Thanks to their vision, Zombies and humans will finally go where no others have gone before.

Mom and Dad for instilling in me an appreciation and acceptance of all creatures—great, small, and infectious.

Illustrator's Acknowledgments

Illustrating this book has been an absolute joy for me; my love of the reanimated deceased is rivaled only by my love of drawing the reanimated deceased. I owe this opportunity to a whole host of people. Thanks to:

Karen and the folks at Adams Media for creating this book and allowing me to be a part of it.

Andrea for thinking of me.

My grandfather who would have loved this book, if only for the fact that my name is on it.

My mother, grandmother, and brother for giving me my sense of humor.

My wife, Beth, for putting up with the aforementioned sense of humor on a daily basis and making everything I do possible.

I'd also like to thank George Romero and Zombies for making books like this possible.